CATS 24/7

Extraordinary Photographs
of Wonderful Cats

Created by Rick Smolan and David Elliot Cohen

CHRONICLE BOOKS
SAN FRANCISCO

Created by Rick Smolan and David Elliot Cohen

24/7 Media, LLC
PO Box 1189
Sausalito, California 94966-1189
www.america24-7.com

Herriot, James. "The Christmas Kitten" from *The Best
of James Herriot*. Copyright © 1982 by Reader's Digest
Assoc. Inc. and used by permission of St. Martin's
Press, LLC in the USA and by Harold Ober Associates,
Inc. for other territories.

"Catch of the Day," copyright © 1999 by Patricia
Schoeder. Reprinted with permission.

Library of Congress Cataloging-in-Publication Data
available.
ISBN 0-8118-4815-9

Manufactured in China

Distributed in Canada by
Raincoast Books
9050 Shaughnessy Street
Vancouver, British Columbia V6P 6E5

10 9 8 7 6 5 4 3 2 1

Chronicle Books, LLC
85 Second Street
San Francisco, California 94105
www.chroniclebooks.com

Pages 2–3
FRESH TURF
Five-week-old Clover explores a field
in Farmington, Minnesota.
Photo by Natalie Gansmoe

This project was made possible through the generosity of the following companies:

PURINA®
Your Pet, Our Passion.™

WEBSHOTS

Lexar™

A®
Adobe

MIRRA™

Google™

jetBlue
AIRWAYS®

GO FISH
Finding Nemo, or in this case Miss Cleo, wasn't the problem for orange tabby Tyson, but getting his noggin into the fishbowl is another story. In the end, Tyson settled for a cool drink over a sushi dinner.
Photo by Elizabeth Zibas

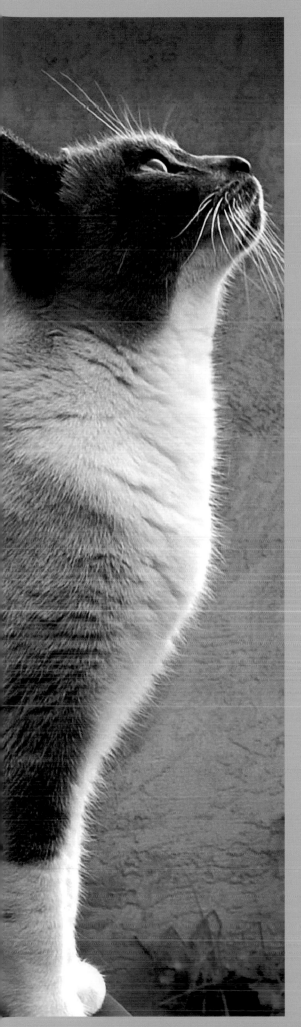

Table of Contents

SUNGAZER
From atop her family's barbecue, Samantha stares at the sun. The rescued stray now has the run of her owners' house. "She's very playful, but also very bossy, and she always chases our dog," says Erin Marsh. "She also insists on sleeping in our bed."
Photo by Erin Marsh

FARM BOY
Iowa farmer Max Schmidt cuddles with his male cat Blossom, named by his granddaughter Abby — who had hoped for a female.
Photo by Charlie Neibergall, Associated Press

TIDY CAT
Fastidious Mojo grooms himself in the bathroom sink and coughs up his fur balls right into the wastebasket.
Photo by Bruce R. Bennett, AOL Member

KIND OF BLUE

Kimberly Wassenberg fell in love with the blue cat with the crooked right ear when she saw him at the pound. The feeling was mutual, and now Van Gogh, a 9-year-old Russian blue mix, guards Wassenberg by meowing whenever visitors approach the house. "He's more human than most humans I know," she notes.

Photo by Kimberly Wassenberg

The Littlest Lion

By Michael Capuzzo

Photo by John Ga nes

The cat, like many great mysteries, is ever two things at once: daylight domestic companion and wild nighttime killer, affectionate cuddler and disdainful snob, beloved pet and despised beast. The cat's essential nature, enchanting to some, infuriating to others, can be summarized simply: The cat does what it desires at all times, no matter what we wish it to do.

Who among us can claim such independence, outside of a criminal, rock star, or god (which, of course, most cats were in previous lives)? Independence and freedom are expected of artists and high-minded revolutionaries, yet these same qualities are problematic when applied to pets. The cat's eternal charm and controversy coexist, as beguiling as the smiling, leering, Cheshire cat in Lewis Carroll's *Alice's Adventures in Wonderland.* "Please, would you tell me, why your cat grins like that?" Alice timidly inquires of the Duchess.

"It's a Cheshire cat," the Duchess replies, "and that's why."

Later, the feline disappears until nothing is left but its grin. It was, Alice exclaims, "the most curious thing I ever saw in my life."

The cat's answer to all of life's questions is as serene and simple as Chinese philosopher Lao tzu's: "Because."

The feline neatly embodies both our civilized selves and our hidden animal natures, and the picture of the big orange tabby sprawled across the suburban breakfast table on page 20 of this book says it all. We are told that Sam goes out to hunt restlessly all night long, granting his family a glimpse of neither tail nor whisker till dawn. But at breakfast he shows up on center stage, taking his place atop the morning paper, and settling in with a serene, cocksure grin.

Clearly, Sam is a master at balancing civilization and an essentially animal nature. In these postindustrial, digital days, we are thick with woeful complaints about our lost humanity. Cats remind us of that which is wild, of unpredictable nature; indeed, they remind us that we are animals, too. The family cat, the contented icon of the sunny household who spends his nights, well, killing small animals, validates our most unexplored yearnings and atavistic dreams. If only our own divided mammalian natures could be so effortlessly and charmingly resolved with the self-satisfied flick of a tail.

Cats, though they hardly deserve it, have long had a reputation as America's most polarizing pet. Their dual nature inspires partisan sniping, eloquent defenders, and a paradox: If cats weren't so persecuted and reviled by some, then perhaps we cat lovers wouldn't love them quite so much. In 1922, in the book *The Tiger in the House*, the New York critic and novelist Carl Van Vechten spoke for cats and cat lovers, writing that "Through all the ages, even during the dark epoch of witchcraft and persecution, puss has maintained his supremacy, continued to breed and multiply, defying, when convenient, the laws of God and man, now our friend, now our enemy, now wild, now tame, the pet of the hearth or the tiger of the heath, but always free, always independent, always an anarchist who insists upon his rights, whatever the cost."

The cat has endured reversals of fortunes in its long life story that would make Dickens blush. Worshipped by the Egyptians some 3,000 years ago, the cat/god cult was so powerful that if a man killed a cat, he was sentenced to death. During Europe's Middle Ages, the shoe was on the other paw: No longer gods, cats became scapegoats, demons even, and were slaughtered by the thousands as witch's familiars. Fewer cats meant more rats; with flea-bearing rodent populations unchecked, an estimated 20 million Europeans died of the Black Death in the 14th century.

Trailing humans around for eons has gotten the cat, who is blithely unaware of his powerful symbolism, caught up in the war between the sexes. Since the age of myth, cats and women have been grouped on the unconscious, intuitive, lunar side of human nature, what Nietzsche called the Dionysian side. To modern sensibilities this may be considered sexist, but remember that the unconscious mind, where cats and nightmares dwell, is also the source of power and creativity. Dogs and men, both coarser pack animals (according to this theory) are left happily yapping in the more pedestrian, daylight world of Apollo. As Robert Heinlein put it, "Women and cats will do as they please, and men and dogs should relax and get used to the idea."

As a syndicated pet columnist for 40 newspapers, I once ventured onto this dangerous ground by reporting an expert explanation that orange cats are almost universally friendly because they are male. Male cats, some animal behaviorists say, are generally friendlier than female cats because, whereas the male devotes his energies to resting and eating like a little lion, the female raises the young and, you know, does everything else. What this may or may not say about humans I will leave for the reader to decide. It is my view that in 21st century society, where the enlightened say we are "owned by our cats," the real power rests with neither human sex.

The family tree of many cat breeds is lost in time, but the domestic cat arrived in colonial America in the ships of European colonists and was prized for its abilities as a mouser. Early Americans were steeped in the practical lore of cats as meteorological aids: A cat on an autumn hearth facing north, for instance, prophesized a long, cold winter.

The mixed-breed cat and the American short hair, with its supple, powerful hunter's body, most resemble the colonial cat. Various other breeds arose, like the husky Maine coon. According to legend, it was bred from raccoons or bobcats, but, in fact, it was selected by settlers for its hardy traits. In the 19th century, Americans discovered more leisure time, and cats became prized as pampered companions. Early prestigious breeds like the Persian and Angora were favored by the rich. The first cat show was held in Boston in 1878, followed by a landmark show at Madison Square Garden, New York, in 1895, presaging "the fancy," or the hobby, of breeding cats into more and more exotic creatures.

While the domestic cat population rose steadily in the 20th century, the great turning point for the cat in the United States occurred very recently, in the last decade of the 20th century, during a time when a cat named Socks reigned in President Bill Clinton's White House. At the time I was doing my pet column. The biggest thunderclap of news I got to report was the fact that cats had surpassed dogs as the nation's most popular pet. The feline triumph had its partisan naysayers: Environmentalists accused the little lion of being an "alien species" that threatened our nation's endangered songbirds. Commentators in the media largely decided the cat boom was a troubling symptom, a side effect: Americans had become more mobile and selfish than at any time in history, they argued. The new mobility required less commitment than your average slobbering, hyperactive Fido demanded—and little more than a bowl of water and a litter box during vacations. The analysis was a slander on the cat/human interface.

"What matters, my friend," the late great animal writer Roger Caras once said, "is that on a planet where most of the life-forms that evolved over billions of years are now extinct, some higher wisdom decided to let people and cats coexist at the same moment in history. What has resulted from that cherished coincidence is a unique kind of love."

Caras, author of more than 70 animal books and the 14th president of the ASPCA, was a famed chronicler of cat stories, like that of Teddy, a stray, a "fat-faced old tom of heroic, even Falstaffian, proportions" who went from attacking every animal it met to living out his years peacefully on Caras's Maryland farm. With love and plenty to eat, Teddy the Terrible morphed into an extraordinarily nurturing father/grandfather figure to three kittens, various mature cats, and several other farm animals. Caras described Teddy entering old age with "a kind of inexplicable wisdom, a resignation, somehow."

"He became a legend-type cat," Caras wrote in his classic, *The Cats of Thistle Hill*, "a living folk song." It is the cat stories we tell ourselves that matter most, he once told me.

"No one should waste their time trying to define mankind's relationship to the cat," Caras concluded in his introduction to my collection of cat stories, published as *Cat Caught My Heart*. "That task defies us," he wrote, "even as cats themselves do.... Love and mystery are practically synonyms in our culture, and cats are just about the most mysterious critters we interact with."

Prize-winning journalist and author Michael Capuzzo has written several books about cats and dogs and, for six years, wrote a weekly syndicated animal column, "Wild Things."

Cat House

SISTER ACT
In their Minnesota house-
hold, resourceful sisters
Flikka and Poppi have devel-
oped some unique skills:
Flikka opens the screen door
with a deft flick of her paw,
while Poppi can pop open
plastic cat food containers.
Photo by Joel W. Sheagren

NOT GARFIELD
The only time Jennifer Newton and her family see Sam, a nocturnal prowler, is when he asserts himself at the breakfast table, usually atop whatever section of the newspaper is in play.
Photo by Jonathan Newton, AOL Member

BEST OF TIMES

Rescued off the streets of Chinatown in 2000, 4-year-old Greta now lives in a big New York City apartment. When not catching up on the headlines, the handsome tabby attacks empty cardboard boxes and lolls in sunny patches on the balcony.
Photo by Andrea Harner

BAD KITTY!

"He's just plain ornery," says Ron Erdrich of Tungsten, a year-old tiger who swats at his owner's legs from underneath furniture and behind doors.
Photo by Ronald W. Erdrich,
Abilene Reporter-News

REAR WINDOW
Outdoor critters—birds, squirrels, chipmunks—
rivet Tango, Samba, and Zildjian. When spring
arrives and Chicago's critters get busy, the three
Tonkinese brothers rarely leave their window
perch.
Photo by Robert Neff

STAR-SPANGLED CAT
Gracie poses in front of owner Jimi Mudd's 32-foot Bristol Bay sailboat, which Mudd and his brother painted to honor Memorial Day in 2001.
Photo by Paul Kitagaki, Jr., AOL Member

HAROLD'S SALUTE
Just outside Sandy Cleary's apartment in Baltimore's Little Italy, a flapping flag taunts Harold, an 8-year-old house cat. There are an estimated 70 million cats living in American households.
Photo by James W. Prichard

HOMELAND SECURITY
Thirteen-year-old sisters Meryl and Jodie stand guard at their Rochester, New York, home. In the past, the well-traveled pair surveilled houses in Michigan and Israel.
Photo by Will Yurman

AQUATIC THIEF

It took Lily several paw swats to convince herself that the bird on the bath wasn't real. Ever since, the finicky feline, an indoor cat who is only allowed outside on leash, has been stealing water from the figurine's live relatives.
Photo by Nancy K. Halstead

POOL BOY

Enduring a scorching west Florida afternoon, Lil' Babies beats the heat. At night, the thirsty 10-month-old paws his owner's bedside glass of water—often soaking the sheets in the process.
Photo by Raven Stone

SLURPY

You can't lead a cat to water, and you can't make him drink. Charlie eats and slurps when he pleases and offers affection to photographer Mirko Scherrer when it occurs to him.
Photo by Mirko Scherrer

ADOPT ME!
Every spring, the cat kennel at the Humane Society of Green Bay, Wisconsin, fills to capacity with strays. The state has an estimated 1 million free-ranging rural cats, whose population swells with each seasonal batch of kittens. The society typically finds homes for just over half of the 4,000 strays it takes in; the rest are euthanized.
Photo by Tim Dardis

SPECIAL DELIVERY
Animals delivered to the Humane Society in Berkeley, California, like these kitties, must "audition" before they're admitted to the no-kill shelter. Staffers reject the biters, barkers, and badly behaved to ensure the animals are prime pet material. Their approach pays off—99 percent of the animals are adopted.
Photo by Lori A. Cheung, www.thepetphotographer.com

SCREEN TEST
Like her namesake wine, Beaujolais is exuberant, young, and surprisingly complex. The 2-year-old ponders life's big questions from behind her screen door.
Photo by Chuck Cass

KITTY LETTER

A neighborhood stray left this 6-week-old kitten on the Tiner's doorstep in Fort Myers, Florida. As soon as she was old enough, the Tiners sent her off, still nameless, to a good home.

Photo by Beverly Carriere Tiner, AOL Member

FEEDING FRENZY
The Crystal Lake, Illinois, no-kill animal shelter is home to about 60 cats and four or five dogs at a time. Each week, around a dozen cats and kittens are adopted into carefully screened homes. In the reception area, which doubles as the dining hall, waiting boarders roam free.
Photo by Juli Leonard

MATERNAL SYMPATHY

Molly, a 3-year-old tabby, and Gertrude McCaffrey bond during the last and toughest days of the cat's pregnancy. Having delivered eight kids of her own (one at a time), McCaffrey sympathizes with Molly's discomfort. Molly had her litter the following morning.

Photo by Steven McCaffrey

NATURAL HEALING
Ninety-nine-year-old Carrie Stidham's steady companion is her cat Jack, who boards with her at the Mountain View Nursing Home. According to studies, a cat's presence reduces blood pressure and calms the heart.
Photo by Doug Loneman,
Loneman Photography

EXTEND-O-KITTY

Cosmopolitan stretches out to full length under the familiar ministrations of owner Vivien Robles in Anaheim, California. All it takes is certain kind of cat—and a feel for feline pressure points.

Photo by Lisa Madary, AOL Member

BABYSITTER

Eleanor, a prickly 3-year-old stray, avoided noisy, grabby infants at all costs until Sophia Milne Kuhn was born. Now, she hovers close to the boisterous babe, willingly offering herself up to tail pulling and ear yanking. "She has become our babysitter," says mom Michelle Milne.

Photo by Michelle Milne

DANDEROUS LIAISONS

Cats and beds may be a natural combination, but for those with cat allergies, the pairing is a recipe for sleeplessness and irreconcilable relations.

Photo by Lisa Marie Iaboni, AOL Member

CAT-A-TONIC

Iowa preteen Sarah Fandel swears 3-year-old Gizmo is the only thing that keeps her sane when she has to get up for school.

Photo by Gary Fandel

OUT OF AFRICA

The ruddy Abyssinian traces its genetic roots to the earlier civilizations of the Nile River Valley. English soldiers returning home from the 1868 Abyssinian War first brought the cat to Europe. Sydney, a particularly handsome example of his breed, follows in his forbearers steps, hunting rodents from a sylvan perch.

Photo by Chris Nelson

RITE OF SPRING

Sparkie strides across his New Hampshire yard toward a flowering crab apple tree

Photo by Victoria Bush

DISPOSSESSED

Ever since her caretaker passed away, Miss Priss (right) has been haunting the Elmscourt apartment complex where he used to live. She often passes by 2 year old Gandalf's window looking for handouts from Gandalf's owner, Michelle Posey. During the winter, Miss Priss finds shelter in the building's laundry room.

Photo by Michelle Posey,
Arkansas Democrat-Gazette

HIMALAYAN AROUND
Because of its snubbed nose, the Himalayan (a Persian and Siamese mix) often has breathing problems. Nine-year-old Kristian is a notorious snorer.
Photo by John Wullschleger

TIGGER TAKES FIVE
Tigger yawns as he settles down for an afternoon nap—on his owners' bed, of course.
Photo by Carol Glaman

BELLY FLOP
"He's a real exhibitionist," says Shane Phillips of 7-year-old Perry. The Blue Devon Rex likes to bear his soft—and rather large—underbelly during naps on his owner's bed or laundry pile. "He's comfortable in his own skin."
Photo by J. Shane Phillips

PEACEABLE KINGDOM
Forty-seven cats and three dogs, all of whom were rescued, reside together in animal rescue volunteer Colleen Feld's Maryland home.
Photo by Laurie DeWitt

LAZY BOY
Homer, like his cartoon namesake, is an unabashed couch potato.
Photo by Albert P. Fuchs,
Fuchs & Kasperek Photography

LET SLEEPING CATS LIE
Don't disturb Little White Kitty when he's snoozing on the deck: He is old and crabby, says owner Justine Olson.
Photo by Justine Olson

Cats Don't Work

COMPUTER MONITOR
While Ginny Fobes Sunde plays with her mom's office assistant, Mike Hipple, Dahlonega guards the computer. "When the cat is around, she thinks we shouldn't work on the computer," says Natalie Fobes. "She swats at us whenever we try."
Photo by Natalie Fobes

STARGAZER
Dusty, named after the cat's affinity for piles of sawdust, wakes up with the first light at Stoney Creek Woodworks in Clarksville, Missouri. When the cabinet shop opens for business, Dusty assumes his regular post in a front window, where he works the strolling tourists.
Photo by Seth Wenig

NIGHT HUNTER

"People think Daphne's lazy because she's always sleeping," says jewelry shop owner Rang Huggins. "But really, she's a survivor." In the wilds of west Texas, rife with coyotes and great horned owls, Daphne, a night hunter, is one of the few cats who have made it to the ripe old age of 4.
Photo by Penny De Los Santos,
National Geographic, Freelance

TELE-TABBY

Art—in this case an *Animal Planet* program—imitates life at a tropical fish supply store in Philadelphia. Seven-year-old Sushi wandered into the shop in 1996 and hasn't left. At her new home, she snacks on koi pellets and laps water out of the fish tanks.
Photo by Michael S. Wirtz,
The Philadelphia Inquirer

TECHNOCAT
Squirt, full-time pet and occasional CPU cozy,
envelops his owner's warm, purring processor.
Photo by Jeff Stoner

SCREEN SAVER
Banished from New York City graphic designer
Maeve Richmond's lap, Telly decided the warm
home-office computer monitor was the next-
best thing. Now, whenever Richmond wants
to read her email or open Quark, she has to lift
Telly's paw—or tail—out of the way.
Photo by David Dadekian

DANCES WITH WOLVES

Two-year-old Claudette perches on a front-end loader at the Loki Clan Wolf Refuge. While the hundred wolf dogs at the refuge might intimidate an ordinary cat, Claudette always stands her ground.

Photo by Lloyd E. Jones, The Conway Daily Sun

TOM CATS

A loyal band of retirees and stray cats, including this fierce calico, mix and mingle over coffee and cat food at a Getty gas station on the Philadelphia Pike in Belfont, Delaware.

Photo by Jennifer Corbett, AOL Member

CAT WITH NO NAME
Barn cats, like this one at Peter Hellwig's Tennessee farm, are so commonplace that their landlords usually don't bother naming them. Like house cats, they live indoors—in barns—but are satisfied with meals of mice and beds of hay.
Photo by A. J. Wolfe, AOL Member

CHECK-IN TIME During his daily romps, ever responsible Monty returns to this cinderblock wall hourly to peer into his owners' house and let them know he's okay. *Photo by Jody Gianni*

SYMMETRY LESSONS Bengal cats are known for their extreme energy, but Favi prefers to lie on the dining room table studying his owner's nursing textbook. *Photo by Andrea Hanssen*

TAKING THE PLUNGE One-year-old tabby Juliette debates whether or not to jump off the roof to escape the magpies dive bombing her from the sky above. *Photo by Stacie Brew*

I'VE GOT MY EYES ON YOU Meg, a feisty calico who sports a metal hip plate from a car injury, still chases squirrels and attempts to surprise butterflies. *Photo by Kira Ravenwood*

THE COMFORTS OF HOME Bubble was abandoned by her mother at 3 days and bottle fed by Lilly Chiang every two hours for the next eight weeks. Now 2 months old, she shows her surrogate mother her appreciation by sleeping on her lap. *Photo by Lilly Chiang*

STRANGE FRIENDS Kit (on floor), Whiskers, and Pidgey (a Quaker parrot) have become best buddies. Early in their relationship, Kit poked at Pidgey's head with her paw, but all it took was a quick peck on the nose to remind her who was boss. *Photo by Christopher Phillips*

LAST STOP LUXURY The Chateau Du Meow in San Diego, California, is an adoption center for stray cats and a permanent home for those with feline leukemia (FeLV) and feline HIV (FIV). FeLV-positive Angela naps in a window seat outside her house, which is equipped with a loft and TV.
Photo by Robin Hart

Catch of the Day

By Patti Schroeder

Photo by Essdras M Suarez, *The Boston Globe*, AOL Member

One night, my 10-year-old cat Rudy got his head stuck in the garbage disposal. Let me tell you right up front that he's fine, but getting him out wasn't easy.

My husband, Rich, and I had just returned from a vacation in the Cayman Islands, where I had been sick as a dog the whole time, trying to convince myself that if I had to feel lousy, at least I was in paradise. We arrived home a day and a half later than planned because of airline problems. I still had illness-related vertigo and, because of the flight delays, had not been able to prepare the class I was to teach at 8:40 the next morning. I sat down to think about William Carlos Williams. At around 10 o'clock in the evening, I heard Rich hollering indecipherably from the kitchen. I raced out to see what was wrong. Rich was frantically rooting around under the sink, and Rudy—rather, Rudy's headless body—scrambled around in the sink, claws clicking on metal. Both were in a panic. I learned later that Rich had tossed a chunk of smoked salmon skin into the garbage disposal, and Rudy (whom we always had called a pinhead) had gone in after it.

It's disturbing to see the headless body of your cat. This is an animal I have slept with nightly for 10 years, who burrows under the covers and purrs against my side, and who now looked like a desperate, fur-covered turkey carcass set to defrost in the sink while it's still alive and kicking. It was also disturbing to see Rich, Mr. Calm-in-an-Emergency, basically freaking out. Adding to the chaos was Rudy's twin brother, Lowell, who raced around in circles, jumping onto the kitchen counter, and alternately licked Rudy's butt for comfort or bit it out of fear. I had to do something.

We tried to ease Rudy out of the disposal by lubricating his head and neck. We tried shampoo and butter-flavored Crisco: Both failed. A now greasy Rudy kept struggling.

Rich decided to take apart the garbage disposal, but couldn't. Turns out, the thing is constructed like a metal onion: You peel off one layer and another one appears, with Rudy's head still buried deep inside, stuck in a hard, plastic collar. My job during this process was to try to calm Rudy, with the room spinning (vertigo), Lowell howling, and Rich clattering around with tools.

I called our plumber, who called me back quickly, even at 11 at night (thanks, Dave). He talked Rich through more layers of disposal dismantling, but still we couldn't dislodge Rudy. I called the 1-800 number for In-Sink-Erator (no response), then a pest-removal service that advertises 24-hour service (no response), then an all-night emergency veterinary clinic (who could offer no advice), and, finally, 911. Rudy's normally pink paw pads were turning blue. The dispatcher offered to send over two policemen. This gave me pause. I'm from the sixties, and, even if I am currently an upstanding citizen, I never considered asking cops to my house on purpose. But the dispatcher was adamant.

The cops arrived close to midnight and turned out to be quite nice. More importantly, they were able to think rationally, which we were not. Astonished by the situation, Officer Mike kept saying, "I've never seen anything like this." Officer Tom, who expressed sympathy for our plight—"I've had cats all my life," he said, comfortingly—had an idea. We needed a certain tool, a tiny, circular rotating saw that could cut through the heavy plastic flange encircling Rudy's neck, and Officer Tom happened to own one. "I live five minutes from here," he said, "I'll go get it." When Tom returned, Rich and the policemen got under the sink to cut through the garbage disposal. I sat on the counter, holding Rudy, trying not to succumb to the surrealness of the scene, with the weird middle-of-the-night lighting, the room occasionally spinning, Lowell's spooky sound effects, an apparently headless cat in my sink, and six disembodied legs poking out from under it. The guys managed to get the bottom off of the disposal; we could now see Rudy's face and knew he could breathe. But they couldn't cut the flange without risking the cat. Stumped.

"You know," Tom said, "I think the reason we can't get him out is the angle of his head and body. If we could get the sink out and lay it on its side, I'll bet we could slip him out." Turns out Mike runs a plumbing business on weekends, and he knew how to take out the sink. They went to work, the three pairs of legs sticking out from under the sink surrounded by an ever-increasing pile of tools and sink parts. They cut the electrical supply, capped off the plumbing lines, unfastened the metal clamps, unscrewed all the pipes, and, about an hour later, voila! The sink was lifted gently out of the countertop, with one guy holding the garbage disposal, which contained Rudy's head, up close to the sink, which contained Rudy's body. We laid the sink on its side, but even at this more-favorable angle, Rudy stayed stuck.

Tom's radio beeped, calling him away on some kind of real police business. As he was leaving, he had another good idea: "I don't think we can get him out while he's struggling so much. We need to get the cat sedated. If he were limp, we could slide him out." The overnight emergency veterinary clinic was only a few minutes away, but we didn't know exactly how to get there. "I know where it is," declared Mike. "Follow me!" Mike got into his patrol car, Rich got into the driver's seat of our car, and I got into the back, carrying the kitchen sink, what was left of the garbage disposal, and Rudy. It was now about 2 A.M.

We followed Mike for a few blocks when I decided to put my hand into the garbage disposal to pet Rudy's face, hoping I could comfort him. Instead, my sweet, gentle bedfellow chomped down on my finger and wouldn't let go. My scream reflex kicked into gear, and I couldn't stop. Rich slammed on the brakes, hollering, "What happened? Should I stop?" checking us in the rearview mirror. "No," I managed to get out between screams, "just keep driving. Rudy's biting me, but we've got to get to the vet. Just go!" Rich turned his attention back to the road, where Mike took a turn we hadn't expected, and we followed.

After a few minutes, Rudy let go. I looked up to discover we were wandering aimlessly through an industrial park, in and out of empty parking lots, past unfamiliar streets. "Where's he taking us?" I asked. "We should've been there 10 minutes ago!" Rich was as mystified as I, but, finally, Mike pulled into a church parking lot and we pulled up next to him. As Rich rolled down the window, the cop, who was not Mike, rolled down his and asked, "Why are you following me?" Once Rich and I recovered from our shock at having tailed the wrong cop car, and the policeman recovered from his pique at being stalked, he led us quickly to the emergency vet, where Mike greeted us by holding open the door, exclaiming, "Where were you guys?"

It was lucky that Mike got to the vet's ahead of us—we hadn't thought to call and warn them about what was coming. When we brought in the sink and disposal containing Rudy, the clinic staff was ready. They took his temperature (down 10 degrees) and his oxygen level (half of normal). The vet declared: "This cat is in serious shock. We've got to sedate him and get him out of there immediately." He injected Rudy, who went limp, then the vet squeezed about half a tube of K-Y jelly onto the Rudy's neck and pulled him free. The whole team jumped into code-blue mode and laid Rudy on a cart, where one person hooked up IV fluids, another put little socks on his paws, another covered him with hot water bottles and a blanket, and yet another took a blow-dryer to warm up his now gunky head. The fur on his head dried in stiff little spikes, making him look pathetically punk as he lay there, limp and motionless.

They sent us to sit in the waiting room while they tried to bring Rudy back to life. I told Mike he didn't have to stay, but he just stood there, shaking his head. "I've never seen anything like this," he said, again. At about 3 A.M., the vet came in to tell us that the prognosis was good for a full recovery. They needed to keep Rudy overnight to rehydrate him and give him something for the brain swelling they assumed he had, but, if all went well, we could take him home the following night. Then, just in time to hear the good news, Officer Tom rushed in, concerned about Rudy.

Rich and I got back home about 3:30. We hadn't unpacked from our trip, I was still intermittently dizzy, and I hadn't prepared my class. "I need a vacation," I said. While I called the office to cancel my class, Rich made a pitcher of martinis.

I slept late the next day and then badgered the vet about Rudy's condition until he said that Rudy could come home later that day. I was working on the suitcases when the phone rang. "Hi, this is Steve Huskey from the *Norristown Times-Herald*," a voice told me. "Listen, I was just going through the police blotter from last night. Mostly it's the usual stuff, breaking and entering, petty theft, but there is this one item. Um, do you have a cat?" I told Steve the whole story, which interested him. A couple hours later he called to say that his editor was interested, too; did I have a picture of Rudy? The next day Rudy was front-page news, under the ridiculous headline "Catch of the Day Lands Cat in Hot Water."

There were some repercussions to the newspaper article.

Mr. Huskey had somehow inferred that I called 911 because I thought Rich, my husband, was going into shock, although how he concluded this from my comment that "his pads were turning blue," I don't quite understand. The first thing I had to do was call Rich and swear to him that I had been misquoted. When I arrived at work, I was famous; people had been calling my secretary all morning to inquire about Rudy's health. When I called our regular vet to make a follow-up appointment for Rudy, the receptionist asked, "Is this the famous Rudy's mother?" When I brought my car in for routine maintenance a few days later, Dave, my mechanic, asked about Rudy. When I called a tree surgeon about my dying red oak, he asked if I knew the person whose cat had been in the garbage disposal. And when I went to get my hair cut, the shampoo person told me the funny story her grandma had read in the paper, about a cat who got stuck in the garbage disposal. Even today, five years later, people ask about Rudy.

The adventure cost $1,100 in emergency vet bills, follow-up care, a new sink, new plumbing, new electrical wiring, and a new garbage disposal one with a cover. The vet can no longer say that he's seen everything but the kitchen sink. I wanted to thank Officers Tom and Mike by giving them gift certificates to the local hardware store but was told that they couldn't accept gifts, and that I would put them in a bad position if I tried. So I wrote a letter to the police chief praising their good deeds and sent individual thank-you notes to Tom and Mike, complete with pictures of Rudy, so they could see what he looks like with a head. And Rudy, whom we originally got for free, still sleeps with me under the covers on cold nights and, unaccountably, still prowls the sink, hoping for fish.

Patti Schroeder is a professor in the English department at Ursinus College in Collegeville, Pennsylvania.

Cats at Play

EN ROUTE
Barnum and Bailey, platinum mink Tonkinese brothers, soak up sun at the Washington State Ferry Terminal. A mix of Siamese and Burmese, the handsome breed is known to be loyal, intelligent, sociable, and willful. *Photo by Tony Overman, The Olympian, AOL Member*

HE'S NAKED!
Gary Baron trains his 6-month-old Sphynx cat, Anubis, at his home in Orlando, Florida. The real estate investor/waiter has taught the clever kitty to fetch, sit up, and come when called. "Because he's hairless, he doesn't throw up hairballs on the furniture," notes Baron. "And he matches the house."
Photo by Ben Van Hook, AOL Member

ONE-ON-ONE

Kayleen Turnis of Bernard, Iowa, spends some downtime with 2-year-old Pookie, her favorite of the 23 cats who live on the family farm.
Photo by Dave Kettering, Telegraph Herald

GOOD KITTY!

Trainer Jennifer Good gives cheetah Sahara a workout at the Cincinnati Zoo. The big, 2-year-old cat instinctually catches the Whiffle ball—and returns it for a treat. A star of the zoo's Cat Ambassador Program, Sahara visits local schools with Good to publicize the problems faced by endangered species.
Photo by Bruce Crippen, The Cincinnati Post

ON THE PROWL
Prowling his own quiet backyard or asleep by the fire, he is still only a whisker away from the wilds.
—poet Jean Burden (b. 1919)
Photo by Will Fandel

COOL CAT
Jason Cook considers 4-year-old Doully to be one of his kids. "Thinks he's human," the Orange, California, father of two says.
Photo by Jason Cook

WHAT'RE YOU LOOKING AT?
"We call her our little porkie," says Ann Harris of her cat Maggie, who is none too happy to have been caught in such an unflattering pose.
Photo by Ann Harris

PHAT CAT

Five years on a low-calorie diet have done nothing to shrink Neko's ample midriff. Perhaps it's because the Russian Blue rarely leaves his upholstered perch in front of the family TV.

Photo by Chad Warner

BELLY BABY

Delilah so loves having her belly rubbed that when her owners come home, she runs ahead of them to block their path before flipping onto her back.

Photo by Christine Stutzman

BUTTERFLY COLLECTOR
Domestic cats hunt less to satiate their hunger than to satisfy their need for physical activity, as this well-fed house cat with a mouthful of butterfly demonstrates.
Photo by Scott G. Winterton,
Deseret Morning News

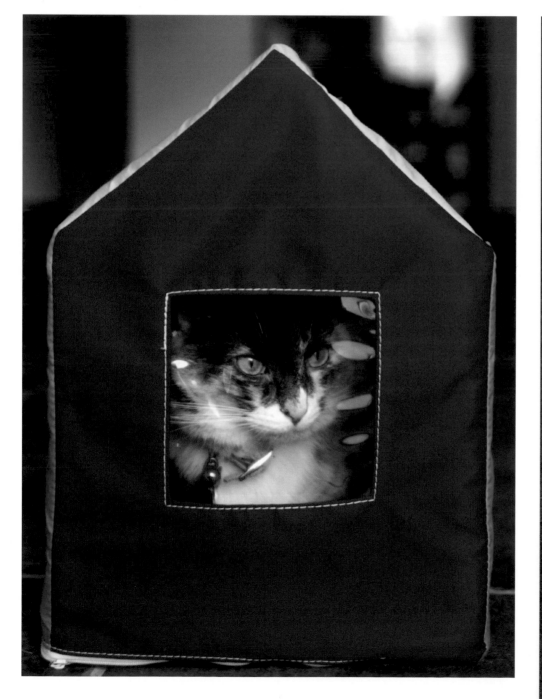

HOME SWEET HOME

Like many cats, 3-year-old Kizzy is claustro-philic—she loves small spaces. If the puss hasn't shown her puss in a while, chances are she tucked herself into this canvas doll-house, taking in the world from her plastic picture window.

Photo by Peter Ackerman, Asbury Park Press

DAY CARE

At an Oregon thrift shop, whose proceeds benefit a feline shelter, the 30 resident cats entertain themselves with whatever donated goods people drop off.

Photo by Ron Winn, AOL Member

TESTING THE WATERS

Mithril, a silver-blue Tiffanie, is a hydrophiliac. He sits on the edge of the bath while his owners bathe. He readily enters the tub for his own shower, and when he's not dirty enough for this privilege, he seeks out new watering holes, like this inflatable pool.

Photo by Rachel Moody

SOMEONE TO WATCH OVER ME

Napster, a mellow cat named for her penchant for sleeping, loves to watch owner Judith Hain's goldfish, which she never manages to catch. "They know her tricks by now," says Hain. "And when they see a shadow, they dive down."

Photo by Judith Hain

THE CATS AND THE HAT
For Midget, a Somali, and JoJo, a Maine coon, the next-best thing to being outside and chasing birds is being inside, chasing the flying fish on Sloane Rickman's coconut-frond hat.
Photo by Rick Rickman

ARISTOCAT

Of New York City's 1.8 million domestic felines, Lulu is one of the fortunate few who have a backyard to roll around in.

Photo by Amanda Schwab

NIGHT VISION

Compared to humans, cats have only 20/80 visual acuity and limited color sensitivity, but superb movement tracking and night vision. As a result, cats see a blurred world of yellow and blue hues during the day and a detailed, active landscape at night.

Photo by Raven Stone

THE CATWALK
During a rare moment of bravery, Scare D. Cat balances on the deck railing of his home in Springfield, Oregon. The 8-year-old was named for his habit of cowering around children and strangers and, after climbing 150-foot Douglas fir trees, getting too scared to come down.
Photo by Nelson Coffman

BATHING BEAUTY Every two weeks, Anna Knox puts her cat Angel on her shoulder and steps into the shower. Angel refrains from scratching by curling into a ball. *Photo by Anna Knox, AOL Member*

TSY BITSY EXPLORER *There is no more intrepid explorer than a kitten.* —Jules Champfleury (1821-1889), French novelist. *Photo by Marie Strange*

JARHEAD When Missy discovered this empty jar, she claimed it, making the five other felines she lives with so jealous that her owner had to get jars for everyone. *Photo by Sharron Paris*

GEORGIE IN CHARGE "She's queen of the roost," says Marshall Warner of Georgie, who keeps an eye on things from her 6-foot-tall cat hutch. "She dominates the dogs and doesn't tolerate a lot of playfulness." *Photo by Marshall Warner*

CAR CAT Dog-lover Amanda Paolino's first cat, Kylie, has a leash and rides in the car. Perched atop Josh Darnell's shoulder, she jabbers excitedly to Paolino. *Photo by Amanda Paolino, AOL Member*

HELLO KITTY Whenever someone says "Hello" to Cameo, she responds with a meow. Her other talent is turning doorknobs to gain entrance to off-limits rooms. *Photo by Joyce Simms, AOL Member*

USE THE FORCE Luke Skywalker listens for the details of his next mission, which he hopes will be carried out near the kitchen and involve investigating a can of Fancy Feast. *Photo by Soo Kim*

WHAT'S GOING ON? Locked in the bedroom while her owner brings home foster puppies, Emma, once a foster pet herself, cocks her head in confusion. *Photo by Rada Miller*

MIXED EMOTIONS

Gabby the cat and Amy the pet mouse
share the same Lexington, Kentucky,
household.
Photo by Dan Brandenburg

STANDOFF

Smithers often catches mice and occasionally goes after a small sparrow, but
he knows better than to challenge the
squawking, aggressive blue jay who
struts in front of his Bountiful, Utah,
house.
*Photo by Rick Egan,
The Salt Lake Tribune*

BUNNY LOVE

Lilly took to Lola right away when the
bunny joined her household. Whenever
Lola hops in from her backyard hutch,
the duo bat around jingle toys and
nuzzle each other.
*Photo by Kimberley Bartolo,
AOL Member*

BACK-DOOR BUDDIES

Most encounters between felines and rodents aren't so civil. But Mandy, a strictly indoor cat, and Split Ear, a backyard squirrel, have managed to bridge a long-standing interspecies quarrel. For eight years, the two have been sharing moments from opposite sides of the Kimmel family's sliding glass door.

Photo by Sharon Gekoski-Kimmel,
The Philadelphia Inquirer

PLAY DATE

Norfolk terrier Eleanor has the run of the Long Beach, California, pet day care grounds. She uses her all-access privileges (she's the owner's pet) to hang out in the cat wing, where she plays with Lil' Joey. Contrary to myth, cat-friendly dogs are fairly common—and 15 percent of U.S. households have both.

Photo by Suzanne Mapes

SCENE STEALER

Benjamin wedges his way into the frame as Paul Sandoz and his friend Whitney Steckel scale the Sandoz's picket fence.

Photo by Gerik Parmele

Pretty Kitty

MOTHER AND CHILD
A month-old kitten basks in her mother's care. Cats are solitary animals by nature—the eight-week period between birth and weaning is one of the few times they live in a familial group.
Photo by A.J. Wolfe, AOL Member

BAD RAP

Associated with superstitions, devils, witches, and bad luck in general, black cats remain the, uh, black sheep of the feline family. Rocky and his pal Sassy are tenants at a no-kill shelter in Kansas. With any luck, Rocky's stay will be brief, and someone will take him home.
Photo by Reed Hoffmann, Freelance

EXPRESSIVE EYES
"When she's angry, her eyes turn yellow," says Alvin's owner, who guaranteed green eyes for this frame by holding up a treat while she shot her photo. Enlarged pupils, which make the eyes appear to change color, represent arousal. But don't look too closely—cats consider staring an act of aggression.
Photo by Kimberly Reed

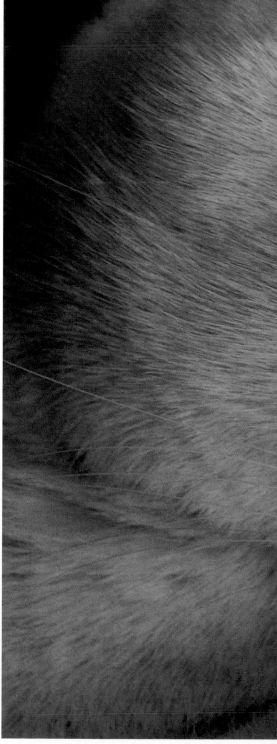

LOVE AT FIRST SIGHT
"We went to get food for our new puppy, and we came back with a cat," says Joan Quaytman, whose daughter fell in love with Jagger and his quiet, contemplative nature the minute she saw him.
Photo by Joan E. Quaytman

NINE LIVES
Miracle had been hit by cars four times when Colleen Feld rescued her and 20 other cats and three dogs (photos on the wall) from a negligent farmer. "I took them all to the vet and had them spayed right away," says Feld, who has since adopted 27 more cats.
Photo by Laurie DeWitt

CONSTRUCTIVISM
Artistic Orson transforms a sheet of discarded plastic into an interactive sculpture.
Photo by Chip Hess

CAT'S CRADLE
Katya has few requirements when it comes to choosing a napping spot. Ideally, it should be warm, square, formfitting—and fragranced with anchovies.
Photo by Shawn-Dana Seitler

FENCED IN

Eight-year-old Duncan spies backyard chipmunks from the outer limits of his roaming area. The indoor Maine coon is also a budding ornithologist, studying bird species of all kinds from the railing of his back deck.

Photo by Essdras M. Suarez, The Boston Globe, AOL Member

IT'S A WRAP

Take one tabby shorthair, roll tightly in a 300 thread count sheet, tuck edges under chin and paws...and voilà! A homemade *purri*to (aka Milo of Detroit, ready for bedtime.)

Photo by Chad Warner

ALLEY CAT
Simba takes a measured, anthropological approach to the birds, cats, and rodents that populate the alleyway next to her apartment. Never one to jump into things, Simba simply observes.
Photo by Jody Gianni

BOOK LOVER
With her wonderful stare, Cleo gazes out the window of The Dusty Bookshelf in Manhattan, Kansas, her bookstore home for the past 13 years.
Photo by Kathryn A. Conrad

BIRD WATCHER
LeeLoo watches birds for hours—before proudly depositing them on his family's Oriental rug. Cats nab more than a billion birds, and 5 billion rodents, in the U.S. every year.
Photo by Ruby Sipes

SHEAR MISERY
Groomer Jennifer Makuta and her assistant Mary James hold down 12-year-old Princess Mimosa (aka, Mimi) for her biannual trim at Veta's Pet Salon in Lexington, South Carolina. Although Mimi doesn't go willingly to her appointments, owner Laura Hudson says the tortoiseshell Persian leaves better prepared for the sweltering South Carolina summers.
Photos by Travis Bell

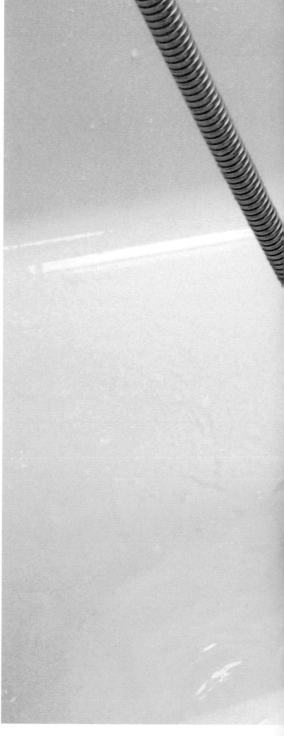

WET 'N' WILD
Mimi cries all the way to and through her one-hour appointment at Veta's salon. A Persian's luxuriant coat easily mats into clumps of tangled hair, especially during shedding season. Biweekly grooming and monthly bathing prevent matting and control dirt and dander.

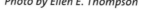

CAT'S EYE

Mr. Jolly's pure white coat and one blue eye are rare—less than 2 percent of all cats exhibit these traits. Unfortunately, his attributes are also strongly associated with hearing impairment. Studies show that 75 percent of white cats with at least one blue eye are deaf, Mr. Jolly included.

Photo by Ellen E. Thompson

BIFOCAL

When 10-year-old Harrigan's right eye suddenly changed color five years ago, spooked owner Tim Nolan called the vet. Harrigan's eyesight was just fine, and the transformation remains a mystery.
Photo by Ashlyn Jones

LUCKY LULU
Lulu had internal injuries, tapeworms, and her tail broken in three places when she was found by the Shea family in 1999. She now lives indoors and sleeps on an orthopedically correct contoured foam bed. At 5 A.M. sharp she wakes her owners with eye and ear licks.
Photo by John Shea

SUN SEEKER
Solitude is hard to come by for a cat living with 14 other felines, 90 Holsteins, and four humans, but this nameless barn cat has found a warm spot for herself on the back deck of dairy farmer Rodney Bailey's house.
Photo by Ruben W. Perez, The Providence Journal

DOOR BELLES
Our house, is a very, very, very fine house, with two cats in the yard.... Two nameless barn cats pose purrfectly at a Rhode Island dairy farm.
Photo by Peter Goldberg, AOL Member

The Christmas Kitten

By James Herriot

My strongest memory of Christmas will always be bound up with a certain little cat. I first saw her when I was called to see one of Mrs. Ainsworth's dogs, and I looked in some surprise at the furry, black creature sitting before the fire.

"I didn't know you had a cat," I said.

"The lady smiled. "We haven't. This is Debbie."

"Debbie?"

"Yes, at least that's what we call her. She's a stray. Comes here two or three times a week and we give her some food. I don't know where she lives but I believe she spends a lot of her time around one of the farms along the road."

"Do you ever get the feeling she wants to stay with you?"

"No." Mrs. Ainsworth shook her head. "She's a timid little thing. Just creeps in, has some food, then flits away. There's something so appealing about her but she doesn't seem to want to let me or anybody into her life."

I looked again at the little cat. "But she isn't just having food today."

"That's right. It's a funny thing but every now and again she slips through here into the lounge and sits by the fire for a few minutes. It's as though she was giving herself a treat."

"Yes...I see what you mean." There was no doubt there was something unusual in the attitude of the little animal. She was sitting bolt upright on the thick rug which lay before the fireplace in which the coals glowed and flamed. She made no effort to curl up or wash herself or do anything other than gaze quietly ahead. And there was something in the dusty black of her coat, the half-wild, scrawny look of her, that gave me a clue. This was a special event in her life, a rare and wonderful thing; she was lapping up a comfort undreamed of in her daily existence.

As I watched, she turned, crept soundlessly from the room, and was gone.

"That's always the way with Debbie," Mrs. Ainsworth laughed. "She never stays more than ten minutes or so, then she's off."

She was a plumpish, pleasant-faced woman in her forties and the kind of client veterinary surgeons dream of: well-off, generous, and the owner of three cosseted basset hounds. And it only needed the habitually mournful expressions of one of the dogs to deepen a little, and I was round there posthaste. Today one of the bassets had raised its paw and scratched its ear a couple of times and that was enough to send its mistress scurrying to the phone in great alarm.

So my visits to the Ainsworth home were frequent but undemanding, and I had ample opportunity to look out for the little cat that had intrigued me. On one occasion I spotted her nibbling daintily from a saucer at the kitchen door. As I watched she turned and almost floated on light footsteps into the hall, then through the lounge door.

The three bassets were already in residence, draped snoring on the fireside rug, but they seemed to be used to Debbie because two of them sniffed her in a bored manner and the third merely cocked a sleepy eye at her before flopping back on the rich pile.

Debbie sat among them in her usual posture: upright, intent, gazing absorbedly into the glowing coals. This time I tried to make friends with her. I approached her carefully but she leaned away as I stretched out my hand. However, by patient wheedling and soft talk I managed to touch her and gently stroke her cheek with one finger. There was a moment when she responded by putting her head on one side and rubbing back against my hand but soon she was ready to leave. Once outside the house she darted quickly along the road, then through a gap in a hedge, and the last I saw was the little black figure flitting over the rain-swept grass of a field.

"I wonder where she goes," I murmured half to myself. Mrs. Ainsworth appeared at my elbow. "That's something we've never been able to find out."

It must have been nearly three months before I heard from Mrs. Ainsworth, and in fact I had begun to wonder at the bassets' long symptom-less run when she came on the phone.

It was Christmas morning, and she was apologetic. "Mr. Herriot, I'm so sorry to bother you today of all days. I should think you want a rest at Christmas like anybody else." But her natural politeness could not hide the distress in her voice.

"Please don't worry about that," I said. "Which one is it this time?"

"It's not one of the dogs. It's...Debbie."

"Debbie? She's at your house now?"

"Yes...but there's something wrong. Please come quickly."

Driving through the marketplace I thought again that Darrowby on Christmas Day was like Dickens come to life: the empty square with the snow thick on the cobbles and hanging from the eaves of the fretted lines of roofs, the shops closed, and the coloured lights of the Christmas trees winking at the windows of the clustering houses, warmly inviting against the cold white bulk of the fells behind.

Mrs. Ainsworth's home was lavishly decorated with tinsel and holly, rows of drinks stood on the sideboard, and the rich aroma of turkey and sage and onion stuffing wafted from the kitchen. But her eyes were full of pain as she led me through to the lounge.

Debbie was there all right, but this time everything was different. She wasn't sitting upright in her usual position; she was stretched quite motionless on her side, and huddled close to her lay a tiny black kitten.

I looked down in bewilderment. "What's happened here?"

"It's the strangest thing," Mrs. Ainsworth replied. "I haven't seen her for several weeks, then she came in about two hours ago—sort of staggered into the kitchen, and she was carrying the kitten in her mouth. She took it through to the lounge and laid it on the rug and at first I was amused. But I could see all was not well because she sat as she usually does, but for a long time — over an hour — then she lay down like this and she hasn't moved."

I knelt on the rug and passed my hand over Debbie's neck and ribs. She was thinner than ever, her fur dirty and mud-caked. She did not resist as I gently opened her mouth. The tongue and mucous membranes were abnormally pale and the lips ice cold against my fingers. When I pulled down her eyelid and saw the dead white conjunctiva, a knell sounded in my mind.

I palpated the abdomen with a grim certainty as to what I would find and there was no surprise, only a dull sadness as my fingers closed around a hard lobulated mass deep among the viscera. Massive lymphosarcoma. Terminal and hopeless. I put my stethoscope on her heart and listened to the increasingly faint, rapid beat, then I straightened up and sat on the rug looking sightlessly into the fireplace, feeling the warmth of the flames on my face.

Mrs. Ainsworth's voice seemed to come from afar. "Is she ill, Mr. Herriot?"

I hesitated. "Yes...yes, I'm afraid so. She has a malignant growth. I stood up. "There's absolutely nothing I can do. I'm sorry."

"Oh!" Her hand went to her mouth and she looked at me wide-eyed. When at last she spoke her voice trembled. "Well, you must put her to sleep immediately. It's the only thing to do. We can't let her suffer."

"Mrs. Ainsworth," I said. "There's no need. She's dying now—in a coma—far beyond suffering."

"Oh, poor little thing!" she sobbed and stroked the cat's head again and again as the tears fell unchecked on the matted fur. "What she must have come through. I feel I ought to have done more for her."

For a few moments I was silent, feeling her sorrow, so discordant among the bright seasonal colours of this festive room. Then I spoke gently.

"Nobody could have done more than you," I said. "Nobody could have been kinder."

"But I'd have kept her here—in comfort. It must have been terrible out there in the cold when she was so desperately ill—I daren't think about it. And having kittens, too—I...I wonder how many she did have?"

I shrugged. "I don't supposed we'll ever know. Maybe just this one. It happens sometimes. And she brought it to you, didn't she?"

"Yes...that's right...she did...she did. Mrs. Ainsworth reached out and lifted the bedraggled black morsel. She smoothed her finger along the muddy fur and the tiny mouth opened in a soundless meow. "Isn't it strange? She was dying, and she brought her kitten here. And on Christmas Day."

I bent and put my hand on Debbie's heart. There was no beat.

I looked up. "I'm afraid she's gone." I lifted the small body, almost feather light, wrapped it in the sheet that had been spread on the rug, and took it out to the car.

When I came back Mrs. Ainsworth was still stroking the kitten. The tears had dried on her cheeks and she was bright-eyed as she looked at me.

"I've never had a cat before," she said.

I smiled. "Well, it looks as though you've got one now."

And she certainly had. That kitten grew rapidly into a sleek, handsome cat with a boisterous nature, which earned him the name of Buster. In every way he was the opposite of his timid little mother. Not for him the privations of the secret outdoor life; he stalked the rich carpets of the Ainsworth home like a king, and the ornate collar he always wore added something more to his presence.

On my visits I watched his development with delight, but the occasion that stays in my mind was the following Christmas Day, a year from his arrival.

I was out on my rounds as usual. I can't remember when I haven't had to work on Christmas Day because the animals have never got round to recognizing it as a holiday; but with the passage of the years the vague resentment I used to feel has been replaced by philosophical acceptance.

After all, as I tramped around the hillside barns in the frosty air, I was working up a better appetite for my turkey than all the millions lying in bed or slumped by the fire; and this was aided by the innumerable aperitifs I received from the hospitable farmers.

I was on my way home, bathed in a rosy glow. I heard the cry as I was passing Mrs. Ainsworth's house.

"Merry Christmas, Mr. Herriot!" She was letting a visitor out of the front door, and she waved at me gaily. "Come in and have a drink to warm you up."

I didn't need warming up but I pulled in at the curb without hesitation. In the house there was all the festive cheer of last year and the same glorious whiff of sage and onion, which set my gastric juices surging. But there was not the sorrow; there was Buster.

He was darting up to each of the dogs in turn, ears pricked, eyes blazing with devilment, dabbing a paw at them then streaking away.

Mrs. Ainsworth laughed. "You know, he plagues the life out of them. Gives them no peace."

She was right. To the bassets, Buster's arrival was rather like the intrusion of an irreverent outsider into an exclusive London club. For a long time they had led a life of measured grace: regular sedate walks with their mistress, superb food in ample quantities, and long snoring sessions on the rugs and armchairs. Their days followed one upon another in unruffled calm. And then came Buster.

He was dancing up to the youngest dog again, sideways this time, head on one side, goading him. When he started boxing with both paws it was too much even for the basset. He dropped his dignity and rolled over with the cat in a brief wrestling match.

"I want to show you something." Mrs. Ainsworth lifted a hard rubber ball from the sideboard and went out to the garden, followed by Buster. She threw the ball across the lawn and the cat bounded after it over the frosted grass, the muscles rippling under the black sheen of his coat. He seized the ball in his teeth, brought it back to his mistress, dropped it at her feet, and waited expectantly. She threw it and he brought it back again.

I gasped incredulously. A feline retriever!

The bassets looked on disdainfully. Nothing would ever have induced them to chase a ball, but Buster did it again and again as though he would never tire of it.

Mrs. Ainsworth turned to me. "Have you ever seen anything like that?"

"No," I replied. "I never have. He is a most remarkable cat."

She snatched Buster from his play and we went back into the house, where she held him close to her face, laughing as the big cat purred and arched himself ecstatically against her cheek.

Looking at him, a picture of health and contentment, my mind went back to his mother. Was it too much to think that that dying little creature with the last of her strength had carried her kitten to the only haven of comfort and warmth she had ever known, in the hope that it would be cared for there? Maybe it was.

But it seemed I wasn't the only one with such fancies. Mrs. Ainsworth turned to me and though she was smiling her eyes were wistful.

"Debbie would be pleased," she said.

I nodded. "Yes, she would...It was just a year ago today she brought him, wasn't it?"

"That's right." She hugged Buster to her again. "The best Christmas present I ever had."

The author of All Creatures Great and Small, *James Herriot (1916–1995) charmed millions with his stories of life as a rural veterinarian in Yorkshire, England.*

Best Friends

BROTHERS IN ARMS
Brothers Jesse Sandoz, 7, and
Paul, 4, have carried 2-year-
old brothers Sam and Tigger
everywhere since they were
kittens. While the big cats
now refuse to be pushed
around the Nebraska family's
farm in baby strollers, they still
relax in the boys' embraces.
Photo by Gerik Parmele

HANG IN THERE, BABY
Not yet feisty enough to scratch, 6-week-old
Rachel allows Spencer Johnson to bare her belly
to the camera. Kittens, who are born blind and
deaf, open their eyes at two weeks, begin to purr
at three weeks, can be weaned at four weeks,
and take their first wobbly steps at six weeks.
They can hiss at birth.
Photo by Bruce Strong, LightChasers, AOL Member

CUDDLE PUSS
Natalie Gildea indulges in snuggle time with Pete the kitten and son Liam on Sunday afternoon, after church.
Photo by Alan Spearman

SOMEONE TO WATCH OVER ME
When Jeanette Aaron was asked to bring something to childbirth class to help her relax, she chose photos of Merlin. The Siamese tabby mix repays the honor by watching over Aaron when she returns home.
Photo by Nick Kelsh

CALICO DREAMS
After a trip to the beauty salon and manicurist, Brittany Breidenbach naps with Sassy before her first prom. The calico's purr helps the Rhode Island teen unwind.
Photo by Bob Breidenbach

COZY CAT

Mot, who was only 3 weeks old when he was found sleeping in the streets of Bacau, Romania, now lives indoors, sleeping between the sheets of his owners' bed.
Photo by Sorin Ionescu

LAZY DAYS

During the winter, Felix and Peaches hibernate on the couch, but in the summer, they head out to hunt in the wilds of their Auckland, New Zealand, yard.
Photo by Vanessa Shaw

ESKIMO KISSES

Mervyn, who was named for the department store he was abandoned in at 7 weeks, snuggles with Havin'. Of the Hansen family's four Newfoundlands, Havin' is Mervyn's favorite, and the two often exchange eskimo kisses.
Photo by Connie Hansen

ODD COUPLE

Skinny Minnie, a former stray cat, darts past Shiloh, a former show horse who was locked in a stall for 10 years so he wouldn't get dirty. The two friends met in 2001 at Winslow Farm in Massachusetts, a shelter for abused and neglected animals.

Photo by Stew Milne

CAT'S CRADLE

At some point, Oreo the barn cat bonded with Randi, a wild mustang from out west adopted by the Reichanadter family of Indiana. Now, every morning the cat follows Randi to the pasture. Randi doesn't seem to mind.
Photo by Jeri Reichanadter

INDOOR/OUTDOOR
Zephyr, whose owners worry that he might take off if allowed outside, glares at his housemate Miss Hitty, who has the run of the neighborhood.
Photo by Stacey Cramp

MISCHIEF MAKERS

Asher and Alby, who were adopted from a litter of stray cats in Kutztown, Pennsylvania, look innocently at the camera. But when not the subject of their owner's photographic endeavors, the 4-month-old brothers ransack the house, toppling lights and chairs.

Photo by Thomas Wolf

FIND THAT SOUND

Charly and his sister Dana, Maine coons residing in Spijkenisse, Holland, listen attentively to locate the sound of the doorbell. "When I come home at night, they stand at the door to tell me the latest news," says owner Hans de Visser. "My wife and I cannot imagine life without them."

Photo by Hans de Visser

HUNTRESS

Diamond takes a break from mothering her new litter. Twelve-year-old Matthew Thompson says Diamond, the bane of squirrels, rabbits, and snakes, would "drag an elephant home to feed those babies."

Photo by Denise Raney

LIFE OF RIELLY

One-year-old Rielly loves to bat college student Kati Cooley's glasses off her nose. "It's his favorite thing to do," she says.

Photo by Dean Riggott,
www.riggottphoto.com

NATURE/NURTURE
Some evolutionary biologists believe humans are hardwired to respond affectionately to mammals that have babyish features (disproportionately large heads and eyes). Kittens, they argue, tap into our innate desire to nurture our young. A 2-week-old calico proves the point, eliciting a kiss from Oregon midwife Sherry Dress.
Photo by Stephanie Yao, The Oregonian

A GIRL AND HER CAT

Hannah Cytron-Thaler, 7, and 9-month-old Gracie give each other Eskimo kisses. When Hannah sets up camp indoors, she puts a pillow at the bottom of her sleeping bag and Gracie crawls right in.
Photo by Shmuel Thaler, Santa Cruz Sentinel

LOVE TRIANGLE

A trio of kitties compete for 6-year-old Esther Buechele's affection on the Valentine Farm in Dubuque County.
Photo by Joey Wallis

SCAREDY CAT

Alicia Jedele cuddles with Syrup, 1 of 15 cats who live on her family's farm in Saline, Michigan. Syrup follows Alicia around on her daily chores, boldly sniffing the pigs, but her confidence—and her ability to stand her ground—quickly evaporates when the pigs respond with bellowing snorts.

Photo by Leisa Thompson, The Ann Arbor News

YOU'RE IT!

With Cooper distracted by the camera, Abby exacts payback on the Cavalier King Charles spaniel. It was high time—mischievous Cooper teases the long-suffering housecat day in, day out.
Photo by Donna Richardson

KISSING LYNX

Aslan, a Canadian lynx, greets volunteer Tim Mull. The 5-year-old cat, who was declawed and kept illegally by his previous owner, is a permanent resident of Rocky Mountain Wildlife Center. Raised on a vegetarian diet, Aslan now feasts on rabbits and roadkill deer, but she still likes the occasional sweet potato.
Photo by Robert Millman

GETTING TO KNOW YOU

Point Defiance Zoo staff biologist Maureen O'Keefe teaches a 6-week-old clouded leopard how to relate to humans. The endangered cats were born in captivity as part of an American Zoo and Aquarium Association's effort to save the species from extinction.

Photos by Tony Overman, The Olympian, AOL Member

WILD AT HEART

Once the leopard cubs mature, they will be placed in zoos instead of returned to the forests of Southeast Asia. Overdevelopment and poaching have destroyed the clouded's native habitat and decimated its numbers. "There's no 'wild' left to return them to," says O'Keefe.

CAST IRON

As far as Jen Loney can figure, it happened like this: Noel was chasing another family cat and knocked into the ironing board, which toppled the iron on him. Noel's cast protects two broken paw bones.

Photo by Nate Billings, The Daily Oklahoman

ALMOST HOME

Tripoli, a three-legged stray, receives some loving from Wayside Waifs supervisor Gayle Morris. The shelter admits 6,000 cats each year and charges a $25 drop-off fee, which enables them to sustain the animals until they're adopted. Tripoli found a home three weeks after she was brought in.

Photo by Tammy Ljungblad, AOL Member

GOLDEN GIRLS
Once feral, Butterscotch is now so comfortable around people that she jumps into strangers' laps the minute they enter the house—and purrs at Samantha Widemark's merest touch.
Photo by Erich Widemark

CAT AND CARRY
Farmer Nerf Sabatine gives Rudy a ride across some of his 100 acres. The 5-year-old tiger has managed to charm the farm dogs who were notorious cat chasers before his arrival. The mules let Rudy rub up against their legs.
Photo by Bridget Besaw Gorman, Aurora

About Our Sponsors

PURINA®
Your Pet, Our Passion.™

Nestlé Purina PetCare Company is proud to sponsor *Cats 24/7* and *Dogs 24/7*, two pictorial testaments to the wonderful role that cats and dogs play in our daily lives. As a leader in the pet products industry, Nestlé Purina PetCare Company is dedicated to improving the lives of cats and dogs through quality nutrition and care. Our core philosophies include promoting responsible pet care, humane education, community involvement, and the positive bond between people and their pets.

In addition to *Cats 24/7* and *Dogs 24/7*, Nestlé Purina is a proud supporter of the American Humane Association. Through programs such as "Very Best Pet Network" and "Pets for People," Nestlé Purina promotes pet adoptions and donates funds and pet food to animal shelters across America. Nestlé Purina also partners with a number of registries and organizations, including the Cat Fancier's Association (CFA), the International Kennel Club (IKC), the American Kennel Club (AKC), and the United Kennel Club (UKC), to support feline and canine enthusiasts at hundreds of cat and dog shows around the country. Nestlé Purina provides strong support to the AKC Canine Health Foundation to advance canine genetics and health.

The Purina Pet Institute is a multi-disciplinary initiative that encompasses Nestlé Purina's Research and Development capabilities, alliances formed with pet care experts across the country, and the Healthy Pets 21 Con-

sortium, a think tank of some of the foremost leaders in pet health and welfare. Healthy Pets 21 focuses on improving pet health and well-being and fostering the quality of pet owners' relationships with their pets. Its goals include promoting responsible pet ownership; raising awareness of issues and advances in pet health, behavior, and well-being; communicating the benefits of the human-pet relationship; and promoting a more pet-friendly society. Nestlé Purina also helps pets live long, healthy, and happy lives through advanced pet nutrition and care studies. At our pet nutrition and care centers in St. Joseph and Gray Summit, Missouri, we conduct studies that contribute to understanding the nutritional needs and feeding requirements of pets. Each year, Purina Dog Chow hosts Incredible Dog Challenge events across the country, culminating in the national championships at the 10-acre Canine Competition Center at Purina Farms. In these competitions, dogs demonstrate their remarkable skills as they strive for the title.

Nestlé Purina offers more than two dozen online Web sites that provide valuable information on responsible pet care, nutrition, and behavior, including Q & A's from veterinary experts, pet health and nutrition news, and fun promotional offers. You can reach all of our Web sites via:
www.purina.com
www.cats24-7.com/purina
www.dogs24-7.com/purina

WEBSHOTS

Webshots is proud to be the official online photo site for *Cats 24/7* and *Dogs 24/7*.

We were eager to use our photo expertise and streamlined technology to power the online photo submission process and introduce our huge community of photo enthusiasts to this exciting new book program. The Pets category of shared photos on Webshots is an extremely popular destination with members viewing over 100,000 cat and dog photos every day.

Webshots, one of the world's largest photo sharing sites, provides consumers with a variety of ways to enjoy and share photos on their computer desktops, TVs, and mobile phones. Only Webshots enables its members to share photos with family and friends through unique features like Photo Messages ™, moblogging, online photo albums, and custom prints and gifts. And only Webshots offers free photo downloads from thousands of professional photos in our Gallery and millions of photos shared by Webshots members in our Community. Wildly popular, Webshots has millions of members who are passionate about their ability to browse the world's largest photo network and use the Web's best photo search.

Webshots, a CNET Networks company, was founded in 1995 and is based in San Francisco, California.

We encourage pet-loving photo enthusiasts everywhere to enjoy the beautiful photos in the *Cats 24/7* and *Dogs 24/7* book series—again and again—and to continue sharing their latest pictures of Fluffy and Fido online all year-round.

Lexar™

Lexar Media has grown from the digital photography revolution, which is why we are proud to have supplied the digital memory cards used in the *America 24/7* series. Lexar Media's high-performance memory cards utilize our unique and patented controller coupled with high-speed flash memory from Samsung, the world's largest flash memory supplier. This powerful combination brings out the ultimate performance of any digital camera.

Photographers who demand the most from their equipment choose our products for their advanced features like write speeds up to 40x, Write Acceleration technology for enabled cameras, and Image Rescue, which recovers previously deleted or lost images. Leading camera manufacturers bundle Lexar Media digital memory cards with their cameras because they value its performance and reliability.

Lexar Media is at the forefront of digital photography as it transforms picture-taking worldwide, and we will continue to be a leader with new and innovative solutions for professionals and amateurs alike.

Special thanks to Olympus, CNET, Digital Pond, Acronym, AOL, Reader's Digest, Catster, Preclick, LaCie, Kompolt Online Auction Agency, and WebSideStory

Adobe

The *America 24/7* series gave digital photographers of all levels the opportunity to share their visions of what it means to live in the United States. This series was made possible by a digital photography revolution that is dramatically changing and improving picture-taking for professionals and amateurs alike. And an Adobe product, Photoshop®, has been at the center of this sea of change.

Adobe's products reflect our customers' passion for the creative process, be it the photographer, graphic designer, layout artist, or printer. Adobe is the Publishing and Imaging Software Partner for the *America 24/7* series and products such as Adobe InDesign®, Photoshop®, Acrobat®, and Illustrator® were used to produce this stunning book in a matter of weeks. We hope that our software has helped do justice to the mythic images, contributed by well-known photographers and the inspired hobbyist.

Adobe is proud to be a lead sponsor of the *America 24/7* series, a project that celebrates the vibrancy of the American spirit: the same spirit that helped found Adobe and inspires our employees and customers to deliver the very best.

Bruce Chizen
President and CEO
Adobe Systems Incorporated

Google's mission is to organize the world's information and make it universally accessible and useful.

With our focus on plucking just the right answer from an ocean of data, we were naturally drawn to the *America 24/7* series. The book you hold is a compendium of images of life distilled from thousands of photographs and infinite possibilities. Are you looking for emotion? Narrative? Shadows? Light? It's all here, thanks to a multitude of photographers and writers creating links between you, the reader, and a sea of wonderful stories. We celebrate the connections that constitute the human experience and are pleased to help engender them. And we're pleased to have been a small part of this project, which captures the results of that interaction so vividly, so dynamically, and so dramatically.

MIRRA

The founding promise of Mirra, Inc. is to help people protect and access their digital photos and files on their PCs with simple solutions that anyone can use, at any time and anywhere. We provide digital peace of mind so you never have to worry about losing life's irreplaceable moments—like family photos and the precious photos in *Cats 24/7* and *Dogs 24/7*. Thus we are delighted to be a sponsor for the 24/7 series. The Mirra Personal Server has made it possible for the editors of these 24/7 books to automatically and continuously protect, back up, and, when appropriate, share 24/7 photos via the Web—including hundreds of photos you see in these books. Kudos to *Cats 24/7* and *Dogs 24/7* for remembering that pets are family, too.

jetBlue AIRWAYS

JetBlue Airways is proud to be the *America 24/7* series preferred carrier, flying photographers, photo editors, and organizers across the United States.

Winner of *Condé Nast Traveler*'s Readers' Choice Awards for Best Domestic Airline 2002, JetBlue provides friendly service and low fares for travelers in 22 cities in 9 states across America.

On behalf of JetBlue's 5,000 crew members, we're excited to be involved in this remarkable project, and for the opportunity to serve American travelers each and every day, coast to coast, 24/7.

Founded in 1995, eBay created a powerful platform for the sale of goods and services by a passionate community of individuals and businesses. On any given day, there are millions of items across thousands of categories for sale on eBay. eBay enables trade on a local, national, and international basis with customized sites in markets around the world.

Through an array of services, such as its payment solution provider PayPal, eBay is enabling global e-commerce for an ever-growing online community.

Thumbnail Picture Credits

Credits for thumbnail photographs are listed by the page number and are in order from left to right.

22 Renea Bosley
Joey Gardner
Lilly Chiang
Krisztina Kiss
Brandon Neal
Mauritz Johansson

23 Lisa Steiner
Susie Spears
Geoffrey Giller
Michael J. Kacmarcik
Chris Shock
Inna Garanina

25 Diane Dick
Andrea Harner
Linda McRae
Colleen Norrman
Ronald W. Erdrich,
   Abilene Reporter-News
Autumn Rupert

26 Lisa Mendez
Reed Lo
Lyle Lukian
Christine Montalbano
G.E. Marshall
Kristen Reed Lange

27 Agnes Vandermeulen
Dawn Abrams
Joan De Lurio
Marlene Scott
Rich Ayala
Kathy Gagliano

28 Jeanne Lieb
Stephanie Yao,
   The Oregonian
Nataliya Khin
Camelia Murgocea
Vikki Hughes
Dawn Sartz

29 Ivy Huen
Stephanie Yao,
   The Oregonian
Anna Knox
Jennifer Jester
Heather Fortnam
Lucia Giannerini

30 Diane Belton
David Peterson
Thomas Ciepluch
Laura Paul
Stacey Taylor
Alix Antell

31 Shlomo Taitz
Cat Nadeau
Michelle Jacobson
Amanda Thomas
Monica Flaherty
Karen Kaleta

34 Aimee Bruckner
Chris Gavette
Kerri Kowal
Paul Kitagaki, Jr.
Laura Hannah
Gloria Bo Yan

35 Erin Colby
Lilly Chiang
James W. Prichard
Shaun McNeill
Kristen Reed Lange
Rochelle Skinner

38 Julie Basten
Nancy Halstead
Joyce Boksai
Thomas Ciepluch
J.W. Wernsen
Stephen Reinhardt

39 Kathy Ronning
Raven Stone
Leslie van Belois
Erin Alexa Sundermeier
Mirko Scherrer
Gayna Carmichael

41 Shanna Eirich
Tim Dardis
Mauritz Johansson
Donna-Marie Burnell
Lori A. Cheung,
   thePetPhotographer.com
Jessica Noles

42 William Bradley
Chuck Cass
Gary Wieland
Evan Bogan
Dean Muzzall
Julian Brookes

43 Leah French
Brian Blair
Beverly Carriere Tiner
Mike McCormack
Sharon Loucks
Vincent Hénault-Brunet

46 Karen Krawzik
Suzanne Nally
Tonya Gresham
Steven McCaffrey
Joanna Curtis
Alix Antell

47 Tricia Jackson
Lori Furbush
Heather Fortnam
Doug Loneman,
   Loneman Photography
Carol Schriner
Larry Zieminski

48 Jodi Lower
Lisa Madary
Jan Crowe
Jody Gianni
Cathy Peterson
Adrian Crossley

49 Jody Gianni
Jan Crowe
Michelle Milne
Susan Stroud
Randy Johnson
Denise Ellison

50 Yumiko Pfantz
Lisa Marie Iaboni
Robyn Turner
Annette Odendaal
Gary Fandel
Jackie Killian

53 Chris Nelson
Lisa Riner
Andy Cote
Victoria Bush
Megan Noble
M.F. Venger

64 Veronica Su
Penny De Los Santos,
   National Geographic, Freelance
Lisa Minakakis
Trisha Sumpter
Erica Murphy
Michael Parisi

65 Mary Kasprzyk
Michael S. Wirtz,
   The Philadelphia Inquirer
Linda Korff
Carrie Bell
Julie Swanson
Dave Pitzer

66 Stuti Bhargava
Jeff Stoner
Eliza Ketchum
Kristi Royalty
David Dadekian
Robyn A Jenzen

68 Karen Moose
Robin Hubbard
Lloyd E. Jones,
   The Conway Daily Sun
Laura Chance
Tammy Alexander
John James

69 Karen Anderson
Kristine Alessio
Jennifer Corbett
Nina Tielenius Kruijthoff
Donna Shaffer
Alejandra Rodriguez

70 Virginia Cathcart
Carrie Kiser
Carol Ho
Heinz Buehler
Ron Winn
Tanya Bennett

71 Connie Foster
Husnu Cakiroglu
Jen Bellanca
Barbara Alper
Holly Kincaid
Reed Lo

72 Lurena Banghart
Chantelle Lidstone
Douglas Kent Hall
J.W. Wernsen
Thomas Ciepluch
Mary Kulik

73 Anna Knox
Alic Wired
Paula Abdilla
Priotniel Amir
Douglas Kent Hall
Teresa L. Trego

76 Katy Giandinoto
Julie Smith
Robyn Turner
Mark Hirsch,
   Telegraph Herald
Julia French
Sharon Mossy

77 Lori Furbush
Cindy Germek
Joe Martini
Kelly Hahn Johnson,
   The Roanoke Times
Michael McLane
Tina McDaniel

78 Laura Scherer
David Grunfeld,
   The Times-Picayune
Amy Wright
Marie Strange
Renato Baldessari
M.F. Venger

79 Thomas Ciepluch
Donna Lempges
A. Marilyn Moloney
Nancy Halstead
Gunes Kocatepe
Arlene Lehman

95 Ainsley KarlCannon
Dave Kettering,
   Telegraph Herald
Stella Hinkle
Jayson Pruitt
Bruce Crippen,
   The Cincinnati Post
Adam Elgressy

98 Amber Santos
Jason Cook
Dan Price
Rebecca Ferraioli
Ann Harris
April Via

99 Laura Paul
Chad Warner
Erika Vercruysse
Mauritz Johansson
Christine Stutzman
Keisha Sansevere

101 Laurie Landry
Dawn Sartz
Jenny DeWilde
Sunny H. Sung,
   The Atlanta Journal-Constitution
Maria Viteritti
Betty Mudd

103 Shelia Vines
Denice Westpfahl
Day Williams
Jeff Turner
Tina Montag
A. Marilyn Moloney

104 Amy Peterson
Peter Ackerman,
   Asbury Park Press
Florence Chan
Deena Roberts
Vincent Hénault-Brunet
Akemi Sannwald

105 Robert Lubow
Ron Winn
John McCoy
Rochelle Clarke
Flea Fletcher
Amy Mills

107 Tiffany Dewley
R Moody
Nicole Charpentier
Sherry Severson
Judith Hain
Chrisoula Edge

111 Dani Rozeboom
Amanda Schwab
Anne Hill
Eileen Smith
Raven Stone
Faye Carter

126 Marinka Hulshof
Kimberly Reed
Jody Gianni
Lynn Andrews
Jenny de Groot
Jacques Smith

127 Weichia Lin
Jens Voü
Karol Tan
Joan E. Quaytman
Paul Neely
Gary Benson

128 Laurie Brookes
Irina Heikkila
Jennifer Posey
Laurie DeWitt
Alain Gauthier
Noga Moon

129 Emily Varga
Chip Hess
Tammy Leber
Soo Kim
Shawn-Dana Seiller
Jenny McCoy

130 Aileen Duffy
Essdras M Suarez, *The Boston Globe*
Aimee Wheaton
Chad Warner
Robyn A Jenzen
Andrew Koshefsky

136 Heidi Bauman
Bernadette Dupuis
Travis Bell
Stephen Reinhardt
Lisa Riner
David Cooper

137 Yolanda Carrillo
Travis Bell
Colleen Norrman
Alic Wired
Stacy Glassburn
Patricia Wright

138 Laurie Brookes
Jon Armstrong
Kaya Savas
Ellen E. Thompson
Jennifer Doffing
Tiffany Hall

139 Katariina Sutphin
Weichia Lin
Marinka Hulshof
Ashlyn Jones
Joan E. Quaytman
Michael McLane

140 Karen Anderson
Amy Rossetti
Michael Brashears
Bernie Cornwell
Kevin R. Wolf
Sandy Farnham

141 Stephanie Tanner
Julie Geiger-Schutz
Marco de Groen
Eric Schecter
Adam Rubinstein
Bethany Sikaras

159 Rick Smolan
Nick Kelsh
Misha Erwitt
Rick Smolan
Alan Spearman
Claudia Ruemmele

162 Sorin Ionescu
Lydie Schouppe
Vanessa Shaw
Laura Olson
Connie Hansen
Tosca van Krimpen

164 Caroline Graeler
Susannah Hill
Stew Milne
Heather Johnson
Gayle LaRue
Bernadette Dupuis

165 Lisa Chadwick
Trisha Sumpter
Jennifer Rotenizer,
   Winston-Salem Journal
Melinda Burch
Tina Montag
Latha Suryaprasad

169 Debi Ayers
Thomas Wolf
MA May
Kim Gelinas
Hans de Visser
Alan Wyand

170 Cathy Gregor
Jonathan Newton
Eliza Ketchum
Merry Williams
William Cavanaugh
Krista Backstrom

171 Paul Gill
Dee Marvin
Suzanne Bohren
Adri van Eijck
Tressa Green
Romi Weiss

172 Aaron Harwood
Denise Raney
Bob Worthington
Dary McIntosh
Dean Riggott,
   www.riggottphoto.com
Myra Reeves

176 Reed Lo
Shmuel Thaler,
   Santa Cruz Sentinel
Anja Bakker
Justin Sims
Joey Wallis
Vanessa Shaw

178 Ilene Rutter
Jan White
Becky Nguyen
Leisa Thompson,
   The Ann Arbor News
Tammy Blackwelder
Amber Santos

179 Debbie Phelps
Nienke Coppens
Craig Armour
Donna Richardson
Carmelynn Cole
Ginny Bishop

180 Alexandre Romeiras
Judith Ragland
Robert A. Makley
Antonio Louro
Bernadette Meegan
Krista Backstrom

181 Denna Harmon
Tony Overman,
   The Olympian
Jody Gianni
Dzejna Valentic
Tony Overman,
   The Olympian
Mark Lagerman

182 Kristine Alessio
Nate Billings,
   The Daily Oklahoman
Deborah Johnson
Yolanda Carrillo
Tammy Ljungblad
Dan Dumitriu

Staff

Project Directors
Rick Smolan
David Elliot Cohen

Administrative
Katya Able, Operations Director
Chuck Gathard, Technology Director
Kim Shannon, Photographer Relations Director
Annie Polk, Publicity Manager
Alex Notides, Office Manager
John McAlester, Administrative Assistant

Design
Diane Dempsey Murray, Art Director
Bill Shore, Associate Art Director
Karen Mullarkey, Photography Director
Bill Marr, Senior Picture Editor
Sarah Leen, Senior Picture Editor

Editorial
Curt Sanburn, Senior Editor
Teresa L. Trego, Production Editor
Lea Aschkenas, Associate Editor
Korey Capozza, Associate Editor
Elise O'Keefe, Copy Chief
Will Hector, Copy Editor

Consultants
Michael J. Rosen
Amy D. Shojai
Dr. Sophia Yin, School of Veterinary Medicine,
   University of California, Davis

Interns
Erin O'Conner
William Cohen
Kara Cohen
Melissa Dulebohn

Morale Officers
Peanut, the cat
Finnegan, the cat

Literary Agent
Carol Mann, The Carol Mann Agency

Legal Counsel
Barry Reder, Coblentz, Patch, Duffy & Bass, LLP

Accounting and Finance
Rita Dulebohn, Accountant
Robert Powers,
   Calegari, Morris & Co. Accountants
Eugene Blumberg, Blumberg & Associates
Arthur Langhaus,
   KLS Professional Advisors Group, Inc.

Web site and Digital Systems
Jeff Burchell, Applications Engineer
Luke Knowland, Designer

Senior Advisors
Jennifer Erwitt
Laureen Seeger
James Able
Maggie Cannon
Brad Zucroff
Megan Smith
Mike Moore
Brian Smiga
Lindsey Kurz
Tom Walker
Pres Williams
Phillip Moffitt
Michael Rylander
Tom Witt
Pete Hogg
Eric Schrier
Tom Ryder
Ted Rheingold
Ted Leonsis
Julie Wainright
Chris Fralic
Martha Danly
Liz Gebhardt
Betty Krause Taylor
Bob Angus
Barry Briggs
Carrie Wiley
Mat Gasquy
Jenny Kompolt
Leslie DuClos
Craig Gauger

Picture Editors
J. David Ake, Associated Press
Caren Alpert, formerly *Health* magazine
Simon Barnett, *Newsweek*
Caroline Couig, *San Jose Mercury News*
Mike Davis, formerly *National Geographic*
Michel duCille, *Washington Post*
Deborah Dragon, *Rolling Stone*
Victor Fisher, formerly Associated Press
Frank Folwell, *USA Today*
MaryAnne Golon, *Time*
Liz Grady, formerly *National Geographic*
Randall Greenwell, *San Francisco Chronicle*
C. Thomas Hardin, formerly
   Louisville Courier-Journal
Kathleen Hennessy, *San Francisco Chronicle*
Scot Jahn, *U.S. News & World Report*
Steve Jessmore, *Flint Journal*
John Kaplan, University of Florida
Kim Komenich, *San Francisco Chronicle*
Eliane Laffont, *Hachette Filipacchi Media*
Jean-Pierre Laffont, *Hachette Filipacchi Media*
Andrew Locke, MSNBC
Jose Lopez, *The New York Times*
Maria Mann, formerly AFP
Bill Marr, formerly *National Geographic*
Michele McNally, *Fortune*
James Merithew, *San Francisco Chronicle*
Eric Meskauskas, *New York Daily News*
Maddy Miller, *People* magazine

Michelle Molloy, *Newsweek*
Dolores Morrison, *New York Daily News*
Karen Mullarkey, formerly
   Newsweek, Rolling Stone, Sports Illustrated
Larry Nighswander, Ohio University
   School of Visual Communication
Jim Preston, *Baltimore Sun*
Sarah Rozen, formerly *Entertainment Weekly*
Mike Smith, *The New York Times*
Neal Ulevich, formerly Associated Press

Essay Writers
Michael Capuzzo
James Herriot
Patti Schroeder

Chronicle Books
Nion McEvoy
Alicia Bergin
Shona Burns
Stephanie Hawkins
Jan Hughes
Tera Killip
Debbie Matsumoto
Deirdre Merrill
Steve Mockus
Doug Ogan
Jay Schaefer
Vivien Sung

Webshots
Narendra Rocherolle
Russ Novy
Diana Donovan
Nick Wilder
Anne Mitchell
Michael Jones
Milenko Milanovic
Andrew Yamashiro
Jeff Boissier
Julie Davidson
Sara Taunton
Penny Adams
Glenn Kimball
Renato Cedolin
Belynda Santos
Corey Herkender
Tara Geear
John Udasco
Teresa Derichsweiler
Martha Papalia

Edelman PR
Nicole Scott
Danielle Siemon

Acronym
Anton Konikoff, President
Tom Rielly, Vice President
Selina Allibhai,
   Search Engine Marketing Manager
Stephanie Hart, Project Manager